A CHORUS OF CHILDREN

Edited by

Becki Mee

First published in Great Britain in 1999 by
POETRY NOW
Remus House, Coltsfoot Drive,
Woodston,
Peterborough, PE2 9JX
Telephone (01733) 898101
Fax (01733) 313524

Copyright Contributors 1999

HB ISBN 0 75430 630 5
SB ISBN 0 75430 631 3

FOREWORD

Although we are a nation of poetry writers we are accused of not reading poetry and not buying poetry books: after many years of listening to the incessant gripes of poetry publishers, I can only assume that the books they publish, in general, are books that most people do not want to read.

Poetry should not be obscure, introverted, and as cryptic as a crossword puzzle: it is the poet's duty to reach out and embrace the world.

The world owes the poet nothing and we should not be expected to dig and delve into a rambling discourse searching for some inner meaning.

The reason we write poetry (and almost all of us do) is because we want to communicate: an ideal; an idea; or a specific feeling. Poetry is as essential in communication, as a letter; a radio; a telephone, and the main criteria for selecting the poems in this anthology is very simple: they communicate.

CONTENTS

A World For The Future

The future is a scary thought.
Will we live? Will we fight aliens or what?
No one knows. It's a puzzle.
Are we facing Armageddon?
Noise, pollution, global warming.
Wars, fighting, terrorism.
Are we ever going to learn
that we must save our planet?
Cruelty, no thought or feelings,
as further species face extinction.
As the guardians of our future
should we not take stock?
People starving, babies crying.
Lack of food and water,
whilst others waste and squander.
Should we not address imbalance?
Mass destruction of rainforests.
Seas where fish no longer swim.
When will man stop and take notice
that Planet Earth is slowly dying?
Hurricanes blow, volcanoes erupt,
as Mother Earth sends us warnings.
Mankind however, seems too selfish, busy,
Is it not time we listened to her?
Politicians talk and posture.
No real solutions do they offer.
Has the time not surely come
for questions to be answered?

The time has come, of that I'm certain,
To stop our race to Armageddon.

Angela Katrina Lucas-Herald

A WORLD FOR OUR FUTURE

What was once a world of beauty
Is now silently dying.
Choking, breathless, dying.
Choked on the fumes of our cars.
Breathless, not enough oxygen.
Dying from traces of humans.

People clamour over peace,
Yet still the wars are fought.
The only race, of all kinds,
Who hungers over death,
rejoices in it, broadcasts it,
is known as 'civilised man'.

America first placed man on the moon,
What destruction will he wreak there?
What country first placed man with peace?

In space, there might be a superior life.
In centuries to come they may whisper

> 'There goes man! The race
> who killed
> his *planet.*'

Helen McLaughlin

A WORLD FOR THE FUTURE

What will the world in the future be like?
Will it be dark, or will it be bright?
What will the world be in the future's day
If we carry on this way?

If we run out of fossil fuel,
If we cannot replace it, what will we do?
And if we should cut down the very last tree
What a sorry place the world would be.

Nuclear power is clean, they say,
But is it really that way?
They say only 2% remains,
But that poisons land, just the same.

Will the world become a barren wasteland?
A world with no trees and flowers and
No ozone to shield us from the sun
And people crying, 'What have we done?'

Or will the world be a happy place
When humanity has won the race
To save the Earth before its end,
By breaking that destructive trend?

So you see, it's up to you,
Whether the world is saved or doomed
For Mother Nature has no voice,
And so it remains, *your choice.*

Catherine Campbell

A WORLD FOR THE FUTURE

So far in the future and yet so near,
There will be no Earth for people to see,
If we keep going on the way we started,
Destroying our planet and all the beauty and wonder it holds.

So we must change our ways and help the planet,
if we are to survive,
And build a new world for future generations,
So our relations far into the future can see
                            all of what we see today.

But what they see will be under no threat,
There will be no pollution or harmful gases,
What they see will be lush green fields and forests,
And man will be living in harmony with all other living creatures.

And maybe this won't just happen on Earth,
But maybe on other planets too!
People living amongst the stars!
How wonderful it would be if it stayed that way forever.

How magnificent it would be to go outside and smell
the fresh air and take a trip into those stars to see your
relatives on a different planet!
And to be able to do that every day of your life
would be just incredible!
And all it takes to be able to do that is to
stop destroying our planet.
I am sure that we can all help to do that and build
a better world for the future.

Caroline Ironside

A WORLD FOR THE FUTURE

Where will we be in a few years' time?
I don't have a clue.
What will the world maybe look like then?
Certainly not like new.

Look at what we're doing to the world,
Us and our fancy cars.
We will be like a different planet,
Maybe even like Mars.

We are ruining the world all the time,
Every single day.
We are damaging the world which is so great,
In every single way.

Keep the world nice for the next generation,
So they can enjoy it.
Just look after the world and keep it clean,
So we can enjoy it.

Kirstin Delaney

A World For The Future

There's only one world, one sky and one sea,
The future of which lies on you and me,
Think of your children and their children too,
What their world's like depends on you.

If you cut down all today's trees,
You're stopping these people from being able to breathe.
Drive round in your cars polluting the air,
You're risking their lives, now that's just not fair!

Think of the future, instead of today,
Provide for the future, then your children may
Live just like us, or hopefully better.
I hope you'll start thinking after reading this letter.

Caroline Selman

IN THE FUTURE

In the future robots will rule Earth.
They will take our minds,
Replacing them with computer chips
So you can't think without
Using a CD-ROM or a floppy disk.

In the future there will be no
Plants or animals,
There will only be robots
And us
Who will be conquered
By the king of the robots,
Killer 2000.

In the future Killer 2000 will be
The most powerful robot
Of them all.
The only way to escape his wrath
Is to run away now
Before it's too late.
So be warned and
Beware!

Hollie Morton (10)

THE FUTURE

The future's dark,
The future's clear,
The future pops in then out of my ear.
No animals around,
They're all out of bounds.
The future's dark,
But still clear,
Will we all still be here?

Amber Coster (9)

THE WORLD OF TOMORROW

Was it abandoned? Is it abominated
Or will it be?
Was it born in love and peace?
Or will it be?

It will be silver or gold
It will be a diamond twinkling
It will be the picture of beauty
It will be loveable and peaceful
It will be scare-free and exciting.

Is this the world of *tomorrow?*

It will be scenic and simple
It will be sterile with style
It will be triumphant
Or will it be?

Janet Ritchie

A WORLD FOR THE FUTURE

As I gazed out the open window
A cool breeze gently flowed
Through the rustling leaves and distinct purple heather,
It floated on and on like an endless line of chimney
smoke being swept up to the clouds.

As I gazed out the open window
The sensations galloped on
Like the luminous sun glowing on every wave
Before my eyes the scenery changed dramatically
into a vision of the world in the future.

As I gazed out the same tightly-shut window
The trees were wilting, the flowers dying.
All that remained were huge long cylinder-shaped funnels
Piping fumes and gases to the heavens.
Computer technology was nearly all that could be seen.

As I gazed out the same tightly-shut window
Not even one human needed to emerge from their site
For all things dull and boring were in a conventional home
As if the world outside had been forgotten like a child's toy.
The greenery and fresh air was replaced with pollution and
unimportant buildings.

The future of the world should be as beautiful as it was
Thousands of years ago but with technology so modern
we can keep it that way.

Charlotte Erdal

A World For The Future

In the future all animals will have homes,
There will be no endangered species,
No bombs will go off,
The world will be a safer place,
Peace in all countries.
All over the world people will see
Lost brothers, sisters, aunties.
No one will be hungry, homeless or lost
'Cause the world will be a better place,
for all of us.

Katy Doig

Boys

Boys are tiring, neat, quiet, silly
And funny but anyway I still like them
They're gorgeous
Sensible and helpful.

They'll cheer you up.
Boys, my dear boys
You are
Really, really fussy
But sometimes you're cool
Just cool, or sometimes

bossy!

Teneshia Robinson

GIRLS

Girls are calm,
Some girls are really posh
With stylish pink toenails
Some girls are kind
But
Girls are hot as pepper,
Girls are always smooth as paper.
Sometimes with hair as long as a rope,
Vivid,
Often motivated and fit,
that's girls!

Asseel Abdul-Rahman (9)

BOYS

Boys are noisy as parrots
Boys are hilarious as jokers
Really crazy like clowns
They're irritating as brothers
Really like football
And are really annoying.

Charlotte Thorpe (8)

BOYS

Boys are as fun as girls
When they hurt people they say sorry
Some boys are naughty
Some are helpful
Others are special friends.

Noor Lawi (9)

GIRLS

Sometimes girls are total fusspots
And always like to get their revenge.
The girls that don't do so much work,
Speak kindly, excitedly and continuously.
Girls always have to be as clean as can be
They just don't like to get dirty.
With some girls
One little touch from a football
And they scream!

Rohan Amin

GIRLS

Girls are annoying
They're nice too
They scream a lot
But my friend likes them (not)
They're teachers' pets but boys are not.
They do this thing called netball
But I still don't like them.
They're careless and I give them
Two out of ten!

Nathan Hall

GIRLS

The girls in my class are grumpy
sometimes they are kind, sometimes not.
But they are bossy
At lunchtime and playtime
Chat, chat, always chat, chat, chat, chat
Got to chat!
Probably because they are shy.
Girls are slow, slow as ants,
Sometimes as fussy as the boys
Girls are like puppets, and turtles too
I can't believe they can chat so much!

Matthew Flynn (9)

GIRLS

Girls have a posh life
Some are fast
Some are slow and
Some are clever.
They are selfish and bossy
But some are good as gold.

Some can be strong or weak
Maybe some might be neat
Some are nice and even messy
Girls have long hair and girls shout.

Sean Atkins (8)

GIRLS

Girls are birds,
Girls have style
But girls are so calm,
Also shy and relaxed,
And always smooth.
Sometimes they are hot as pepper.
The best girls are a gang of vivid dancers.
Some girls are motivated in gymnastics.

Bhavesh Mistry (8)

GIRLS

Sometimes girls are like clumsy hyenas
And they don't do as much work.
They speak excitedly, politely and continuously
They play silently and perfectly.
Girls are noisy as parrots
And they are hot as chilli pepper.

Davan Wan (8)

BOYS

Boys are as much fun as our climbing frame
As confusing as words
They walk as happily as the sun
Boys are monkeys, jumping up and down
As naughty as my brother
They run as quickly as cheetahs
Boys are kind, but a little bad
Boys are as noisy as chatterboxes
As slow as a turtle
Boys are as quiet as a clock
Tick-tock, tick-tock!

Nafizah Bashir (8)

BOYS

Boys, boys, say to me
'You are just like me'
Boys, boys, so nervous, so fussy,
Not always so nervous
But cheerful and helpful.

The boys in my class.

Yasmin Darrox

SISTERS

Sugar and spice,
And all things nice,
That's what they say,
They are made of.

But I have a sister
And Brogan's her name
She screams all day,
And plays Barbie games.

She fusses and whines,
When things don't go her way,
She stamps her feet,
When you don't want to play.

She has names for her dolls,
Like Blossom and Paul,
With frills and ribbons,
They drive you up the wall.

Sugar and spice,
And all things nice,
When Brogan's around,
You'll pay the price!

Joseph Clements (9)

GIRLS ON BOYS - WHAT I THINK

I have to say,
To make my day,
To express my thought,
On boys that are short,
On boys that are thin,
On boys that are fat,
All of them
Are just scaredy cats.
They make you want
To burst into flames.
Their silly remarks
But they ain't ashamed.
On the other hand,
There are the girls,
With cooing voices
And hair with curls.
So what do you think?
Which one's the best?
The girls of course
There's no contest!
Can't you see
They're really nice
So kind and sweet
With their fashionable clothes
And their elegant feet.
Who's the best?
The girls go up
The boys go down.
Come girls,
Let's leave the 'clowns'!

Vanessa Kelly

GIRLS ARE MY FRIENDS

Girls are my friends,
We play together,
Sometimes football,
Depending on the weather.

Girls are my friends,
We play together,
Today, tomorrow,
Forever and ever!

Nick Selvadorai (8)

GIRLS ON BOYS

Boys are a pain in the neck
They beat the rest
But we can beat
The little old cheats
And still be the best.

Some boys are cute
Some boys are evil
They always think
They're the brainiest people.

Nicola Murrant & Kimberley Thomas

GIRLS

Girls are as shy as mice
They skip so fast
That you couldn't miss a thing.
Girls are chatty parrots
They are as funny as a comedian
And as calm as a snail.
They're fussy
Sometimes annoying
And tricky.

Nathan Gentles

GIRLS

Girls are brainier than boys
But boys say they are dumb.
Girls are ugly and independent
They like to sing a lot and dance.
Some girls are ticklish
And some are playful.
Girls are hyenas.
Girls are good.

Kareem Chouiki (8)

GIRLS

Girls are silky like cream
And stylish like pink tutus.
Nice as dolphins
Jumpy as gazelles
Brainy like Brain Duane Scientist.
Girls are a gang of vivid players
I think they are irritating
It's a funny thing in their world
They are a bit violent somehow
I like my sister
I like my mum
What a story!

Ashkan Ahangaran (8)

Boys

As far as *friends* go,
Boys can be quite nice,
But sometimes they are rude,
And often don't think twice.

As far as *boyfriends* go,
I like them quite a lot,
Sometimes they are babies,
And normally talk such rot.

As far as *brothers* go,
They really are quite mean,
Most of the time they're horrible
But sometimes can be keen.

As far as *general* boys go,
They mainly are okay,
But some days I hate them,
And that day is today!

Laura Newman

GIRLS

The girls think they are strong,
But it doesn't last very long,
They wear quite a good dress,
But they always eat egg and cress.
Scarves they wear for which their mothers pay
But they all lose them in a day,
They can't run around a tennis court,
That is why they are bad at sport.
All they can do is cook,
Also they can read a book.
They can't do a simple sum,
I don't want to show this poem
                    to my mum.

Pratheesh Puvanagopan

BOYS

What I wonder is, are boys as nice as girls?
But really I think girls are better.
Boys are pains and really dumb,
But some boys are sensitive and sweet
But some just a pain. I've got a brother,
Sometimes sweet and nice, but a pain.
He's just like other boys.
I wonder why, don't you?
I like some boys, I hate some boys,
They're the boys that do farts.
A friend of mine that's a boy, went to Jupiter,
Came back looking stupider.
He did a fart, went on a cart and said
'Who's done a fart?'
But hey! What do I care as long as
                                    I'm a girl.

Sarvenaz Oraee

GIRLS

Some girls are good.
Some girls are bad.
Some girls are happy.
Some girls are sad.

Some girls like music.
Some like magazines.
Some girls like dancing.
T-shirts and jeans.

Some girls are horrible,
Calling rude names.
Running round the playground
Playing rough games.

Dean Roberts

GIRLS ON BOYS

Boys can be a pain in the neck
And their bedrooms can be a total wreck.
They leave their homework to the last day
And they don't seem to finish it anyway.
Their excuses are always bad
Because they blame it on their dad.
Football is all they're interested in
I wish I could poke them with a pin.
I hate boys as you've sussed out
Why are there so many boys about?

Carly Harris (11)

BOYS VS GIRLS

Some girls are quite nice
They will help you with your work,
And if you get stuck
They won't call you a jerk.

But when you get to know them better
They will try to take advantage
By burning us down with their good looks,
Our one disadvantage.

Rhys Romo (10)

GIRLS

Boys are simply drowned in words like,
Does my bum look big in this?
Are you sure I haven't got too much make-up on?
I don't look fat, do I?
But boys can only say one thing,
Of course you don't, you look stunning tonight.

Daniel Trickett (10)

BOYS ON GIRLS, GIRLS ON BOYS

Boys and girls are very different.
Boys are strange and annoying.
They always find ways to stress you.
They think they rule you,
They don't, but they want to!

Girls on the other hand are pleasant and beautiful.
They dress well and are kind,
But some girls annoy boys as much as boys annoy them
Although the boys don't seem to mind.

When boys fight they use their fists
But girls can be just as bad.
Saying hurtful words, being cruel
And making each other sad.

So now you see that we are very different
With our habits and our silly ways
And if we get into a fight,
It could last for days.

Well, this is my opinion on boys and girls.
I don't know what yours is.
You can tell who you want, if you want to
But I don't think it will be the same as this!

Ashley McEnaney (10)

THE BOYS

Rough and tough
That's the boys

Rude and in a mood
That's the boys

Grubby and dirty
That's the boys

Disgusting habits
That's the boys.

Elizabeth Ret (10)

WATCH OUT! WATCH OUT!

Watch out! Watch out!
There are girls about
Swishing and swirling
In a girlish way.

Watch out! Watch out!
There are boys about
Running and tumbling
Like thugs in a gang.

Watch out! Watch out!
There are boys and girls about
Playing kiss chase
Oh no, one of the girl's got a boy!
Kiss! Kiss! Kiss! Kiss!

Matthew Hanks (10)

BOYS

Boys are useless
in every way
all they do
is sleep, eat and play.
They drive me crazy
why?
Because they're lazy.
It amazes me
how tired
they can be
after doing the hoovering
or just cooking the tea.
They think they're great
for doing a chore of two
but they're nothing more
than
the muck
on the bottom
of their shoe.
Most *boys*
are football-crazy
and just think
because we are girls
we can't play
and there's no way
they'd let us anyway.
They are most probably scared
in case they get beat
because some girls are pretty neat
I think *boys* are overall freaks.

Camella Davis

CAN'T LIVE WITH THEM; CAN'T LIVE WITHOUT THEM

Girls are a pain in the neck, that's what I think of them,
They always do nothing when you tell them to do something.
I have a sister who thinks she's the best,
She always pinches me on the bum and laughs.
When she starts a fight with me she always chickens out,
But I chicken out when she gets her feet out,
Because her feet smell worse than a drain; Now that's bad.
The only girls I like are my mum and my girlfriends,
They're really nice to me, unlike my sister.

Terry Oliver (10)

BOYS! BOYS! BOYS!

Boys! Boys! Boys!
They make so much noise,
They love to play
With their favourite toys
They never like to
share them.
Us girls just can't bear them
but even so we will still
care about the
annoying
Boys! Boys! Boys!

Chemaine Constant (11)

Bad Boys At Christmas

Bad boys
Bad boys
Decorating a tree,
On Christmas Eve.

Bad boys
Bad boys
Cannot get to sleep,
They want to go and
See the presents under
Their Christmas tree.

Bad boys
Bad boys
Hear the bells
Ringing at midnight,
Hush! Hush!
Now go to bed.

Bad boys
Bad boys
All asleep.

Santa, Santa
Comes and goes
Leaving bad boys
All alone.
They're too naughty -
Off he goes!

Bad boys
Bad boys
Are
Good boys now!

Good boys
Good boys
All around
Waiting for Christmas
Next year round!

Charandeep Singh Chhokar (10)

BOYS

Boys are so lazy,
They'd drive anybody
Crazy!
They always like to fight.
I know that,
Because they talk loudly
In the night.
They always snore
And they're such a bore.
They are always playing
With a ball.
They'd drive anybody
Up the wall!
Boys are just so
Awful!
But my brother-
He's the best!
Well - he's better
Than the rest!

Helen Monsurate (9)

BOYS ON GIRLS

When I was younger
I thought boys were yucky
Because they used to steal my 'sucky'.
They used to pull my hair
And act as if they didn't care.
Why were they so mean?
Killing little animals
For the fun of hearing them scream!

Boys like girls
Who give them twirls
And are not shy
Talking to a guy.
You say 'I love you'
I say 'Boo-hoo-hoo.'

Girls like boys
Who win them toys
And have been invited over for tea
But not when they fight over me.

Alisha McKenzie (12)

GIRLS YES, BOYS NO!

Girls I like
Boys I hate
Girls have got crazy taste
Boys make a lot of noise
When they play with their toys.
Girls are nice
Boys are bad
I don't know, I don't care
Boys are dumb.
I care, I want to know
Girls are great fun!

Gemma Marr (9)

Boys

They stink,
They embarrass me pink,
They're all mad about football,
And most of them are too tall.
They think they are so cool,
But they end up drowning in
The pool.
They think they're best at everything,
When they can't even sing.

Sarah L Picot (10)

THE DAY WE MET

I'll never forget
the day that we met
the moment I saw you
My target was set.

We went to a movie
You said it was groovy
I asked what you wanted to eat,
you weren't choosy.

We went for a stroll
You fell down a hole
And I had to help you get out
with a pole.

We went to the park
And as it got dark
You got scared by a dog
when it started to bark.

I walked you home
and broke your mum's gnome
We talked about the
millennium dome.

You shut the door
And I finally saw
I didn't want to see you
any more.

So don't try and phone
'Cos I won't be home
We're not an item now
You're on your own.

Ryan Pidgen (13)

GIRLS ON BOYS

Boys are unfair,
They think girls are only good to do the housework,
They say girls are better at it than them.
Is this just an excuse because they're lazy?

Why can't girls play football?
'Because they're girls,' they say,
'What's wrong with girls?' we say,
Then they're stuck for words.
Boys are unfair.

Daisy Hogan (9)

GIRLS ON BOYS

Boys are such a pain in the neck.
They are rough, tough and always naughty.
Some are great to have around,
the ones that aren't so bad.

When it comes to Valentine's Day,
they really are a pain.
They will ring you up and
talk for hours and hours.
About in a month's time,
Dad comes up with this great, long, massive bill,
and says that you are grounded.
No more TV. Great!

What else can go wrong now?
Mum comes dashing into my room and says
'What have you done to my make-up and beautiful dress?'
I told my mum that I had to go to a disco.
Mum is very angry indeed.
Now I am in big trouble again.

Good job I have something to occupy myself.
Delicious brown chocolates lie on my clean white bed.
I stuff myself with these lovely chocolates all through the night,
curled up into a ball, listening to all the sounds.

I really do hate boys.
They are so annoying.
The world would be better without a single boy.

Priya R Khugputh (10)

GIRLS ON BOYS

Oh yuck!
What an infamous piece of muck!
Why boys were created, I don't know,
Maybe they were created just to be low,
Boys are thick,
They make me sick!
All they think of is football, football, football!
Which is so horrible, horrible, horrible!
Boys are gross,
They're all morose,
But it makes me shudder,
To know that to become a mother,
A boy I'll have to marry,
The eggs I'll have to carry,
Which will hopefully produce girls,
Pretty and beautiful as pearls.
But boys shall have to be near,
Or girls wouldn't be here,
Oh dear!

Natalie Dixon (9)

GIRLS ON BOYS

My opinion on boys,
Has turned completely around,
I used to say 'I hate them,'
And never want them around.

Then one day at my primary school,
A sweet boy asked me out,
When my parents questioned me,
I denied it without a doubt.

Then I thought I was in love,
Holding hands all day long,
A few weeks later he dumped me,
Oh what had I done wrong?

Many cute boys at high school,
Caught all of my attention,
I dated quite a few of them,
No one special enough to mention.

And then about a year ago,
My friend showed me this lad,
Tall, dark hair and gorgeous eyes,
I liked him really bad.

He's sweet, funny, romantic and kind,
I'm glad we got together,
And now I've fallen in love with him,
I hope it lasts for ever.

Amanda Pearce (16)

BOYS!

Some boys are fun,
Some boys are dumb!
Some boys are clever
But boys *whatever!*
Some boys are bliss
Some boys *kiss!*
Some boys are handy,
But some like brandy.
Boys may have spanners,
And some hold lots of banners.
Some boys are vain,
They play a silly game.
Boys think they are funky,
But they act like a monkey.
Boys are for sale,
But listen to them wail!
Do they ever stop?
And their Pringles go *pop.*
They are very stupid,
Like they've been shot by Cupid.
They'd like any weather
Even if their name was Heather.
Boys like to play football
Even in a shopping mall.
Boys like PlayStations
On a train desk of information.

Jenna Pickering (10)

GIRLS

Some girls are pretty
they are very cheeky,
lots of girls I hate
and sometimes they are late.
They wear lots of make-up
and they never ever wake up.
Girls are boring
they're worse at snoring.
Some girls are small
and can't kick a ball.
Some girls have germs
and they look like worms.
Girls hurt and pinch
and they really do stink.
Girls really slap
and make you sit on their lap.
I hate girls
because they always tell.

Addison Levens (10)

Boys, Who Needs 'Em?

There is one question I must shout,
It's what a boy's life is all about.
To watch TV, to waste their cash
or to sit inside and eat bangers and mash.
Boys are dipsticks boys are dumb
and lie when smells come out of their bum.
Boys are dumb as well as stupid
and fall in love as if they've been shot by Cupid.
If a boy had one million brains
his working standard wouldn't be the same,
it would be worse, but that's natural, of course.
Boys think they're tough and hard and cool
but really all they do is drool.
Boys are fickle, boys are thick,
they have a brain the size of a tick.
Boys just don't get it, they haven't got a clue,
so I'd like say something on behalf of all the girls.
'Boys, who needs 'em!'

Alexia Papaspyrou (9)

BOYS

Fair or dark,
you'll find them in the park.

You will see them playing with their mates,
often chasing girls for dates,

They never wash behind their ears,
and when they're older they like to drink beers.

On the computer they spend their time,
instead of enjoying the sunshine.

They like getting dirty,
and with their mums they all get shirty.

They pull your hair,
without a care.

They read their comics,
during home economics.

Love or hate them,
we all choose to date them.

In the end we marry,
and their babies we carry!

Sophie Mclachlan (9)

BOYS - WORST CREATION ON EARTH!

I've wondered why the heck,
boys are such a pain in the neck!
Boys have had an arrow shot by Cupid,
that is dumb and stupid!
They should be kept in a herd,
when they're learning to become a nerd!
If there is a fight we tell a chum,
while they go crying to their mum!
Boys act like they have lots of toughness,
but when they face us it's real roughness!
They act like they're really cool,
but it is we who really rule!
Boys should be locked up in jail,
naughty and sneaky, that's all about a male!
They go to a stupid college,
while we girls are full of knowledge!
They say their favourite subject is PE,
but it is really, of course, the TV.
Boys like to show their hairy chest,
but *ugh!* Give me a rest!
On behalf of all the girls boys are
The worst creation on Earth!

Clare Bendall (9)

MAYBE - MAYBE NOT

Some boys are not that sad, but some are really bad.
Some are a hit but mostly a miss,
My general view is why girls don't like boys, they're not that crazy!
If boys got more knowledge and all went to college it would be okay.
Most of them don't swear, but some of them act like grizzly bears.
Some say their prayers, but some don't even climb the stairs.
I would like a boy to have nice hair, and eat lots of pears.
I would like him to have a big part in a play and be in school to stay
If they always say 'Hi' then no way!

Kavita Raja (10)

GIRLS

Girls are really mad girls are really sad.
Girls aren't always sugar and spice but
sometimes they can be really nice.
Girls play lots of girly things and wear
lots of sad rings and things.
Boys are cool, some girls act the fool.
Some girls are bright and others start a fight.
Girls are really sad.

Ryan Duffy (9)

BOYS ON GIRLS

Girls are always fussing,
And smell of Christmas stuffing,
Girls should be banned,
And never own some land.
Boys are the best,
Better than the rest.
Boys play football,
And never play netball.

Aaron Clayton (9)

GIRLS

Girls always think they are the boss of you know what!
When they fall over in the playground, they scream and shout!
They spend valuable time deciding what pen,
pencil, rubber and ruler to use!
They spend half their lives wearing make-up, and
the other half deciding what colour eye shadow to use.
To put it plainly and simply
They are indecisive in every single way!

Still what would we do without them?
Love them I suppose.

Marcus Bond (9)

BOYS

Boys
always run
around. Boys, boys
pick their noses. Boys
are always messing
around. Boys, boys.
Mischief is their
middle name.
Boys
are always playing football.
Boys play with Action Man.
Boys have small brains. Boys
think they're cool and tough
but they're not!

Victoria Estruch (8)

GIRLS

Girls think they are tough,
half their life they put on make-up.
They are fussy about their clothes.
Girls think they know everything and they
giggle like babies.
You know boys are the greatest!

James Dixon (9)

GIRLS ON BOYS

Short, fat, thin or tall,
When boys are with girls they are having a ball.
Acting tough, acting cool,
Trying to make that special girl drool.

When girls are not around boys don't care,
They can do whatever they dare!
They might sing or even dance,
Around their bedroom they will prance.
But when girls appear,
Their faces are full of fear!
Will they be gentlemen?
Will they impress?
Will they be annoying pests?
Or will they laugh at the way we are dressed?

Boys and girls are not the same,
Girls are kind and some quite tame.
Boys are loud and always fun
We girls love at least one
Some are cool some are sad
But boys are not really all that bad!

Lynne Carter (12)

GIRLS ON BOYS

Over the messy macaroni cheese,
The *cool girls* smile and wink,
While the *sad girls* glare and whisper,
Over the other side of the hall . . .
Or so it is in *their* minds.

The *sexy girls* slink over,
And join in the laughs and fun and smiles,
While the *tomboy girls* glare and whisper,
Over the other side of the hall . . .
Or so *they* think.

But suddenly the tables are turned
And the boys lose interest in the *tarty girls*
While the *energetic girls* whisper and slyly glance
Over the other side of the hall,
Or so *the boys* think.

The next day:

Over the dry beefburgers,
The *sporty girls* smile and wink
While the *trying-to-be sexys* glare and whisper
Over the other side of the hall . . .
Or so it is in *the boys'* minds.

Seonaid MacLeod

BOYS

Boys can be fun
and sometimes really dumb
they are sometimes quite sweet
occasionally hard to beat.

They fall out of bed
looking almost dead
come late into class
after falling asleep in the bath.

They wear scabby old clothes
covered in dirty old holes
they laze around the house
like a sleepy old mouse.

They are so disorganised
and never apologise
their hands are so grubby
like a little teletubby.

They spend all their money
on big jars of honey
they sleep on the mat
curled up like a little cat.

I have come to the conclusion
that boys are just an intrusion
boys are all the same
and we refuse to take the blame.

Leanne Trotter (12)

BOYS

Strutting down the street in their gangs,
You start to inch away,
But once they've seen your face,
And called your name,
You have to play your part,
By saying 'Hi' or 'How are you?'
When you wish they'd just not ask,
But without boys in your life,
No jokes, no laughs, no fun,
So they are good to have around,
Even if they can be dumb.

They sometimes can be cool,
With their looks and jokes,
And their 'feel good' clothes,
Some look cute,
Like Leo D,
And others with good jokes,
Like Chandler on TV.

Anna Hammond (13)

GIRLS ON BOYS

Boys can be bright and funny,
Cool or maybe not
They are smart and they're sexy,
Knowing all about football!
That will get them into trouble
Or maybe even a fight
But they will never learn.
They can use us and abuse us
Or be charming and just right
They think we'll never beat them
Playing football throughout the night.
If you tell them that they're wrong
They'll always say they're right.
But in the end
You will find
You can't live with them
And you can't live without!

Zoë Marshall

GIRLS ON BOYS

The thing about boys is you don't know what to think of them,
They've all got names like girls do, like Fred, Josh or Clem,
Some smell, some don't,
Some wash and some won't.
Some boys are big some small,
And some don't like girls at all,
But some are nice looking, intelligent and those,
Are much better than ones that just pick their nose,
But boys can be sensitive they're not just rough,
Dirty, smelly and tough,
They can get quite nervous and concerned at times,
And I'm not quite sure if this poem rhymes!
Some boys are swots,
And some just know lots,
About football and things like that,
Anything to do with a ball, basket or bat.
But the thing about boys is,
You can't live with them but you can't live without them,
And boys will always be boys,
And girls will always be girls.

Nike Osifodunrin (12)

GIRLS

Girls go to Rainbows,
Boys go to Beavers.
Girls wear bows,
Their favourite flower is a rose.

Girls are bossy,
Girls are fussy.
Girls buy everything they see.
Girls wear skirts and blouses,
Boys wear shirts and trousers.

Girls go to Guides,
Boys go to Scouts.
Girls are tall,
Girls drive me up the wall!
Girls have long hair.
Girls seem to be everywhere!

Steven Franklin (10)

GIRLS

Every girl is silly and is bad,
They are dumb and they are annoying
and they're really mad.
Gemma's bossy but also mad.
So is Deborah and boys are glad.
Why are girls made again, may I ask, why?
If I don't know I will die.

Stefano Perdoni (9)

GIRLS ON BOYS

Dirty foul disgusting creatures,
These are some of their main features . . .
Kicking a football big or small.
Writing rude comments on the wall.

These dirty foul disgusting creatures
Have to have something good about them said
So all I can say is
They give our world character in a whizz.

Fiona McCallum (12)

GIRLS ON BOYS

We girls are just so kind and gentle,
Boys on the other hand are totally mental,
Well, that's not completely true,
Not all boys have the feelings of a shoe.

Some can be charming, caring and funny,
But most are just obsessed with Segas, cars and money,
Boys can be nasty and really mean,
So be careful you don't become too over-keen.

Sometimes girls fall out over small, silly things,
I admit we don't always deserve our bright angel wings,
If you think boys are not very nice,
Listen to the rule - 'Always think twice!'

Anjela Datta (12)

GIRLS ON BOYS

Now let's start off with an introduction to our lovely friends - *the boys*,
they love footie, they're the next Alan Shearer, but when they score -
the noise!
No, we can't moan all the time, let's talk about our 'soon to be men'
because you've got to admit, yes you've got to admit that you really
really love them!

Number one boy, not our favourite you know, he's the *brainbox* who
knows A to Zed,
he's distinctly remembered for his swotty swot glasses and egg-like
shape of his head.
You'll normally find him in the library, sticking his nose in a book
with small print,
which causes eye strain which is the reason he blinks when he's
thinking, I think!

Boy number two - he's the *good looking guy* with the extremely
white glistening teeth,
he's our knight in shining armour, our tarzan you know, and the girls
always fall at his feet.
He is the 90s Danny Zuko, with the leather jacket who sings love songs
under the moon,
just to think of him you're in paradise, just to think of him - *swoon!*

Then there's client 'Numero tres', the *new age greenie* -goodness me,
he's a dweeb,
he'll save anything from a molehill to a mountain, from a big
oak tree to a seed.
He's the boy standing during his lunch break outside with a poster
saying 'Save the Whale',
He'll save anything, anywhere, any time, any planet, sun, sleet,
rain, thunder, hail!

And last but not least, there comes the *wimp*, the last boy, the worst
boy, number four,
Even if he loses a charity match 5-6, you can guarantee he'll come
crying to your door.

The wimp bleats, rather than speaks, blames others never
himself, of course,
But even if you tell him to go away 'cos he's moaning, you'll
make him even worse!

So sorry boys if you're listening to this, we don't mean to be so mean,
You're really cute and soft inside all the time, gut sometimes you can
be really obscene.
You try to show off all the time, but it doesn't impress us - only
apart from a few,
the only thing we want from you is you, yes you and only 100% of you!

So my fellow girls, now do you see that most boys aren't fab
just sometimes trouble,
but try not to be too mean to them, don't try to burst their bubble.
So give these four types of boy a go, why not try first with a
rating out of ten?
Because you've got to admit, yes you've got to admit that you
really love them!

Stephanie Jane Coe

GIRLS ON BOYS

What is there to say about boys?
Well, they are usually short, dorky and make loads of noise
They sit on their bums and they grin the whole day
But you can't help but love them, there's no human way.

Some are funny and are always in trouble
But nothing can depress them or burst their bubble
When they go, it makes you cry
And you miss them more as days go by.

They always try to impress you
By acting all macho and cool
But the truth of the boy and his pals
Is that they can't stand to be whipped by us great gals!

Some boys are small and real geeks
They think all us gals are pretty weak
And want us just as *girlfriends*
But then we have the pleasure of kicking their rear ends.

There are always the class clowns
Like these two guys called Cob and Ross
They may not be too smart
But they are always ready for a lark!

But what I am about to say
Is something you should know
No matter how much we scream, yell and say 'We hate you!'
We just can't live without you.

Lucie Phillips (12)

GIRLS ON BOYS

I wonder what boys think of in those little heads of theirs?
Football and trainers - do they really have no cares?

Surely they must think of clothes, shopping and music too?
And surely they must find girls gorgeous. Come on, wouldn't you?

I wonder what boys think of when they lie in bed at night?
Do they ever think of the future and meeting Mrs Right?

Do they really spend their lives standing round in baggy clothes?
Playing football, watching TV, fighting . . . who knows?

I wonder what boys think of, I really cannot see.
I think of them all the time, but do they ever think of *me?*

I wonder if boys spend hours perfecting every curl?
Do they know they're talked about by every decent girl?

I wonder what boys think of in those little heads of theirs?
Football and trainers - do they really have no cares?

Kate McLaren (12)

Boys

Boys are as irritating as an itch,
Boys are hilarious.
They are as terrible as lions.
Sometimes they are polite and kind.
They always play football.

Candace Toppin (8)

GIRLS

Some girls are good,
Some girls are bad.
Some smell nice,
Some smell bad.
Some girls are bright,
Some girls are dumb.
Some are from heaven,
Some are from hell.
Some girls are funny,
Some girls are sad.
Some girls are thin,
Some girls are fat.
Some girls are pretty,
Some girls are not.
Some girls are clean,
Some girls are messy.

Robert Morrow (9)

GIRLS

As beautiful as the sea,
As boring as science,
As bright as rocket scientists,
As motivated as a pack of wolves,
As interesting as computers,
As much fun as board games,
As intelligent as hungry lions.

Girls are playful monkeys,
Girls are swift seagulls.

Girls are like sly crocodiles,
Girls are like pink tutu.

Girls are great.

Morgan Taper (8)

BOYS

Every day wherever I go,
I see those strange things,
They never go.
They play rough and tough.
They scream and shout.
They haunt you, they frighten you,
They try to kiss you *ugh!*
I've always wondered what the strange things are.
I guess I'll never know until the time comes
When I give birth to one of these things that play with toys
They are called
Boys!

Hayley Sullivan (12)

GIRLS ON BOYS

Girls are better than boys, we do not:
Ignore you when you talk,
We do not watch rugby all day,
And
We girls never leave the toilet seat up!
So
Over all boys are just so annoying,
They never tidy up,
They never cook,
So
Now do you see us girls do
Everything
So
Girls are better than boys.

Holly Taylor (12)

BOYS

Boys are friendly
Boys are bossy
Boys are forgetful
Boys are cheeky
Boys are funny
Boys are bad-tempered
Boys are untidy
Boys are shy
Boys are crazy
Boys are clumsy
Boys are unusual.

Sarah Al-Tahan (9)

MALE?

Pssst! What is it?
Is it legal . . . ?
Violent!
Our opposite
Sporty
Mad
Boy.

Samantha Nattress (11)

Boys

Boys I hate
They make a lot of noise,
They break girls' toys,
Boys are bad,
And very sad,
And I wish they would all go away.

Deborah Larkin (9)

GIRLS

G irls are giggly and silly
I hate them sometimes.
R eading magazines and painting their nails.
L aughing and whispering, they really are a pain.
S isters especially are the *pits!*

Dean Hall (11)

BOYS

Boys are inquisitive
They can be inquisitive sometimes,
Inquisitive means nosy
It's nearly all boys!

Boys are fabulous
Well some boys.
I like boys who are fabulous,
Boys can be fabulous at times!

Boys are weird
They hold spiders in their hands,
Pretend to hold worms,
Put mud in their mouths,
That's so weird!

Boys are romantic
They give you flowers,
Help you with your work,
If you're in trouble, say they did it.

Onysha Collins (8)

A WORLD FOR THE FUTURE - ENDANGERED EARTH

The Americans have got them
The French have too
Got nuclear bombs
Boo! Boo! Boo!

Nuclear reactive
Nuclear waste
Nuclear bombs
Not my taste!

Nuclear reaction
All around
No life anywhere
To be found

Some plastics
Elastics too
Destroy the ozone layer
But should you!

People getting hot
Because of the sun
The destruction of the ozone layer
Has begun

The ozone layer
Dwindling away
The earth getting too hot
For us to stay

When the ozone layer
Is gone
Earth's population
Equals . . . none!

Simon Haigh (11)

THE FUTURE (MY SCENE)

Buses, aeroplanes, trains?
No! No! No!
Space shuttles, spaceships, space rockets are more my scene.

Burgers, chips, pizzas?
No! No! No!
One tablet three times a day is more my scene.

Oxford Street, Regent Street, Kings Street?
No! No! No!
Mars, Pluto, Venus are more my scene.

Doctors, nurses, dentists?
No! No! No!
Exchange shops for new body parts are more my scene.

Washing, cleaning, ironing
No! No! No!
Robots are more my scene.

So come on let's go to the future and have some fun!

Trisha Meera Mistry (10)

SCHOOL!

School school, who needs school
School is boring, school is too early in the morning.

Why is school on a week day
Why is school in May?

School school, who needs school
School is boring, school is too early in the morning.

Who needs school when you can go to the
Movies instead!

Nabaloga (9)

A World For The Future

A world for the future,
      For me would be,
Less shops, more trees
      More honey and bees.
More forests and woods,
      And animals wild and free.
A war-free place,
      Less illness in our race,
No more famines,
      No more pollution,
No more drugs,
      We need a solution.
My future world would be complete,
      When all of this is done,
Then at last we could perhaps, all live as one,
      On this great globe a bit smaller than the sun.

Elisa Buttle (12)

A World For The Future

Pollution we need a solution.

      Fumes from our cars
      are danger at large.

Factories expel a nightmare
from hell.

      CFCs have got to cease
      if we want to have some peace.

Beaches unclean becoming obscene.
Lying in the sun is no longer fun.

      The water we drink is not as clean
      as we think.

Future, what does it hold
for someone like me?

Charlotte Dodds (9)

ELIMINATED

In the future I expect the world will be a
different place.

The towns will be full of floating cars.

No pollution will fill the air.

People will no longer walk upon the streets
because gangsters will rule the paving.

Houses will run on solar panels and animals will
be found only in parks and zoos.

Josh Childs (9)

A WORLD FOR THE FUTURE

Wild animals will soon be gone
If road builders have their way
One day they're there, the next they're not
So listen to what I say

Stop cutting down trees
Stop shooting animals
And don't pollute the air
And for goodness sake most of all
The ozone layer must be there

As the world gets hot and the sea rises
House by house disappears
Soon the world will be gone
People will begin their tears.

Nick Lee (10)

A WORLD FOR THE FUTURE

The world is full of fear and disaster
Death is all around us.
Pollution all nearby,
Destroying the earth.
Lives lost,
Because of what we leave.
Soon all will be lost.

With progress this could stop,
New lives beginning.
Clean, fresh air.
Peacefulness around us.
Nothing lost,
And nothing wasted.
Soon it *will* be better.

Michael Myers (10)

STOP AND THINK

People chopping down trees
Soon there will be no air to breathe

People don't care about trees
Nor the land, nor the seas.

Lots of animals getting killed
Into the sea sewage is spilled

All the fish will soon be extinct
Because people don't seem to think

So sit down talk it through
Before it's too late for me and you.

Nicola Clark (11)

A WORLD FOR THE FUTURE

What will happen in the future,
Multicoloured chocolate bars,
Maybe children driving cars,
Spend our holidays up on Mars,
Go to Jupiter and all the rest.
Our parents, doing their best
To put our planet back to its best.
Restoring our forests,
Cleaning the seas,
All that is in the future,
Just you wait and see.

Claire Robertson

WHERE IS MY FUTURE?

What have all the grown-ups done
to spoil all my fun.
Too many cars and all the fumes
makes me ill much too soon.
Can't they see what they have done
to me and all the little ones.
Where is my future
is there one?

John Burns (8)

BLINDFOLD

You walk on because it's none of your business
It's someone else's life
Out of the corner of your eye you see a gun,
But it's someone else's wife.

You go home and unlock the freezer,
Lift out your heart
The phone rings and you listen blankly
To someone else falling apart.

She tells you how he hammered her face,
Of the love that ended in pain
But you can't help thinking it's someone else's loss
And someone else's gain.

On the news, in distant countries
A hundred massacred, dead,
But the time it takes to get through traffic
Is all that's in your head.

You walk on because it's none of your business
It's someone else's life,
Out of the corner of your eye you see a gun
And a bullet in your wife.

Tamsin White (17)

SUBMISSIONS INVITED
SOMETHING FOR EVERYONE

POETRY NOW '99 - Any subject,
any style, any time.

WOMENSWORDS '99 - Strictly women,
have your say the female way!

STRONGWORDS '99 - Warning!
Age restriction, must be between 16-24,
opinionated and have strong views.
(Not for the faint-hearted)

All poems no longer than 30 lines.
Always welcome! No fee!
Cash Prizes to be won!

Mark your envelope (eg *Poetry Now)* **'99**
Send to:
Forward Press Ltd
Remus House, Coltsfoot Drive,
Woodston, Peterborough, PE2 9JX

OVER £10,000 POETRY PRIZES
TO BE WON!

Judging will take place in October 1999